FIREFIGHTING
IN WILTSHIRE

An Illustrated History

ROD PRIDDLE

TEMPUS

For Tony 'Arch' Canvin

First published 2008

Tempus Publishing
The History Press
Cirencester Road, Chalford,
Stroud, Gloucestershire, GL6 8PE
www.thehistorypress.co.uk

Tempus Publishing is an imprint of The History Press

British Library Cataloguing in Publication Data.
A catalogue record for this book is available from the British Library.

ISBN 978 0 7524 4515 1

Typesetting and origination by The History Press
Printed in Great Britain

Contents

Acknowledgements

I would like to thank all of those who kindly provided photographs for inclusion in this book and whose names appear in the captions. Where photographs appear without credits, these are from the author's collection.

Andy Groves MA MSc LLB (Hons) FIFireE, Chief Fire Officer of Wiltshire Fire & Rescue Service, has given approval and support for the book, and I wish to express my appreciation to him and his staff for the help I have received from them. I am also grateful to the following who have contributed by accommodating my requests: ADO Graham Ridley, Stn O. Keith 'Jimmer' Flippance, Stn O. Graham Littlefair and Sub O. Jason Hampshire of the Defence Fire & Rescue Service, Nigel Bundy, Danny Hicks, Dennis Hill, Rodger Hyslop, George Johnson, Dick Lardin, Neil McConchie, Graham Myatt, Norman Parker, Pete Rivers, Mike Stone, the late Mike Tatem, Peter Thorpe, Chris Trimby, Neil Trussler and Andy Wright.

Vehicle Abbreviations used in the text:

ATV: Auxiliary Towing Vehicle
EP: Emergency Pump
EST: Emergency Salvage Tender
ET: Emergency Tender
HP: Hydraulic Platform
PE: Pump Escape
TL: Turnable Ladder
WrT: Water Tender
WrT/E: Water Tender Escape
WrT/L: Water Tender Ladder
WrL/R: Water Tender Ladder Rescue

Introduction

Wiltshire Fire Brigade was one of the 141 brigades formed on 1 April 1948 under local authority control as a result of the introduction of the Fire Services Act of 1947. Albert V. Thomas was appointed the first Chief Fire Officer. The various individual brigades, which became part of the National Fire Service from August 1941, were absorbed, with some villages losing their units and having fire cover provided by a nearby station within the authority. *Firefighting in Wiltshire* is published to commemorate the sixtieth anniversary of the formation of Wiltshire Fire Brigade, but is also a pictorial record of the late nineteenth- and early twentieth-century brigades and the equally important private, industrial and military units which have provided valuable services in protecting life and property from fire in the county.

Over the years numerous industrial companies have provided their own fire brigades, as there were insurance benefits in such provision. These brigades have ranged from providing a single manual appliance to having fire engines equal to those of the local authority. Vickers Aircraft Company at South Marston, Pressed Steel in Swindon, GWR/ British Rail in Swindon, Pains Wessex Fireworks at High Post, Westinghouse Brake & Signal Company in Chippenham and Avon Tyres in Melksham are just a few examples of post-war industrial brigades. The latter, now known as Cooper Tyres, is one of the survivors and an important part of the county's fire defence. It is affiliated to Wiltshire Fire & Rescue Service and responds to the same emergencies when required, whether these are within the factory or out in the county.

Wiltshire has a long association with the military, primarily the Army and the Royal Air Force. The Army Fire Service had stations at Bulford Barracks, Tidworth Barracks and at Netheravon Airfield, the base of the Army Air Corps. A number of airfields have been in use by the RAF during and since the Second World War, with each having its own fire section. The Defence Fire & Rescue Service now provides fire protection at military establishments and the various locations of these sites in Wiltshire are covered in these pages.

The county of Wiltshire covers a large area, with its towns, villages and the city of Salisbury located on the periphery of the 200sq. miles of Salisbury Plain. The county has not suffered any of the boundary changes imposed by post-war.governments. Due to this rural expanse, Wiltshire Fire & Rescue Service relies heavily on retained personnel to man its eighteen retain stations. Swindon, Stratton and Salisbury are the sole 24-hour manned stations. Westlea, Chippenham, and Trowbridge are day-crewed but out-of-hours personnel respond when alerted by pager.

On 1 April 1948 Wiltshire Fire Brigade's first emergency call was to a fatality, when Flt Lt L. Taylor RAF, flying a Spitfire from the Empire Flying School at Hullavington, crashed at Kingston St Michael. A fuel leak caused an engine fire and, whilst attempting to land at the airfield, the pilot lost control, overshot the runway and dived into the ground. There have been some noteworthy fires throughout the county, with the market town of Marlborough having had its share of serious incidents. The town has the widest main street in the county, providing good defence from fire spread, and this has been successful. Unfortunately, lateral spread between the terraced properties has resulted in a number of serious fires.

The town sits on the edge of Savernake Forest in which the US Army had an ammunition store during the Second World War. An explosion occurred there in 1945, and there was a far worse explosion the following year involving an ammunition train in the railway sidings used to supply the stores. The NFS from surrounding towns attended both emergencies and, as a result of their actions at the train incident, the company officer from Marlborough and a section leader from Ludgershall were awarded the George Medal. A section leader and fireman from Marlborough and a fireman from Ludgershall received the MBE. A serious fire at the Polly Restaurant in the main street in July 1966 involved the rescue of two children and their grandmother from the upper floor. Three Marlborough firefighters received the Queen's Commendation for Bravery. There cannot be many rural towns whose firemen have received as many bravery awards.

The role of the firefighter has changed considerably throughout the twentieth century and will continue to do so into the future. There have been occasions when Wiltshire's firefighters have been called upon to assist in serious incidents outside the county boundary. During the Second World War, as a result of bombing raids, crews and appliances were deployed to, amongst others, Birmingham, Bath, Bristol, London and Plymouth. In the long, hot summer of 1976 Salisbury and Amesbury crews tackled fires in the New Forest, Marlborough provided cover for a number of days in Reading, and Stratton did the same in Slough. Ramsbury and Stratton attended the Windsor Castle fire on 20 November 1992, and crews from Stratton responded to the serious flooding in Gloucestershire in July 2007.

Terrorism is the current threat to stability in the UK, with the transport system and major cities seeming to be prime targets. Wiltshire Fire & Rescue Service is well equipped to deal with the aftermath of such acts whether they occur in the county or beyond.

one

Early Town
and Village
Brigades

Old Fire Engine, Malmesbury.

This manual fire engine, housed in St Giles church, Great Wishford, is the oldest in the county and possibly in the country. It was built by Richard Newsham, a pearl button maker from London, and purchased by the churchwardens of Wishford Magna in 1728 for £33 3s 0d. (Wiltshire Fire Brigade Museum)

On 24 August 1777 disaster struck Aldbourne when fire virtually destroyed the town. As a result, two manual fire engines were purchased in 1778 from John Bristow, Engine Maker, Ratcliffe Highway, London. The larger was christened 'Adam' and the smaller 'Eve'. They were used until 1924 when a Stratton St Margaret manual Pump was purchased at auction for £27 10s 0d. 'Adam' and 'Eve' survive in the parish church. The Fire Engine House, built close to the church in 1867 at a cost of £26 8s 1d, is still in existence today. (Wroughton History Group)

In 1807 the village of Avebury purchased a manual fire engine from Hadley & Simpkin of Long Acre, London, at a cost of £79 5s, paid in cash. The Pump was refurbished in 1892 with the names of the then-churchwardens added in place of the originals. The Pump attended many fires over the years and was still operational in the Second World War when it was 135 years old. Fire brigade personnel from around the world will have encountered this Pump when attending courses at the Fire Service College at Moreton-in Marsh, where it is displayed. (Wiltshire Fire Brigade)

This manual fire engine was described as 'new second hand' when purchased for Bishopstone Fire Brigade in 1905. The officer-in-charge of the brigade at the time was Captain John Povey. (Wiltshire Fire Brigade Museum)

Swindon Fire Brigade's steam fire engine attending a fire at Blunsdon Abbey on 22 April 1904.
(Wiltshire Fire Brigade Museum)

This scene followed a fire at the Great Western Hotel in Swindon on 29 July 1913. The fire gutted
the hotel garage destroying a new hearse, a new Shillibeer, a brougham, two motor cars, four bicycles,
a quantity of fur coats and mackintoshes, tools and tyres, at an estimated cost of £2,000. (Wroughton
History Group)

Swindon Borough Fire Brigade personnel and equipment at their Cromwell Street fire station, *c*.1922. The motor vehicle is thought to be their converted Lorraine-Dietrich open-top touring car, adapted to carry two men on each side plus the driver and officer-in-charge. (Wiltshire Fire Brigade Museum)

Swindon Borough Fire Brigade in 1925 with a Dennis Pump Escape, purchased from Skurrays Garage in Swindon for £1,403 in December 1923. Pump competitions were very popular at the time and Swindon personnel were considerably successful, as can be seen from the trophies. (Wiltshire Fire Brigade Museum)

The Borough of Marlborough Fire Brigade with their manual Pump outside the new town hall, *c.*1902–05. When a new motor fire engine was supplied to Marlborough by Merryweather & Sons Ltd in 1926, the company took this manual Pump and allowed the council £15 in exchange. (Wiltshire Fire Brigade Museum)

The Borough of Marlborough Fire Brigade's motor fire engine supplied by Merryweather & Sons Ltd in August 1926. It had a Hatfield 250 gpm reciprocating pump, 30 gallon water tank, 180ft hose reel, fifteen 100ft lengths of hose and a 35ft ladder at a cost of £1,100. Chief Officer H.V.L. Kelham wrote to Merryweather & Sons in February 1927 listing details of fires attended with the Pump and praising its qualities. (Bath Record Office)

In the parish of Chippenham Fire Brigade, this Merryweather manual fire engine was purchased in 1849 for £96, following a public appeal for donations. The appeal raised £154 from sixty-nine contributors, including nine insurance companies. The engine and firemen are seen beneath the Chippenham railway arches on Brunel's Paddington to Bristol line. (Wiltshire Fire Brigade Museum)

Captain Joe Buckle, chief officer of Chippenham Fire Brigade, with his crews after a fire in a cloth mill at Westmead Lane on 21 May 1915. At the time this was probably Chippenham's worst fire, resulting in the complete destruction of the mill. Joe Buckle was a local businessman who was well known throughout the county. He served as chief officer from 1914–34. (Wiltshire Fire Brigade Museum)

The parish of Chippenham Fire Brigade in 1899 at the railway arches, which were used for storing the escape ladder. The 'Fire Engine House' at that time is thought to have been in the market place. (Wiltshire Fire Brigade Museum)

This steam Pump was purchased for Chippenham Borough Council Fire Brigade in 1902 and the escape ladder was bought in 1905. The Pump served in Chippenham until 1922 when it was sold to Melksham Fire Brigade for £200. (Wiltshire Fire Brigade Museum)

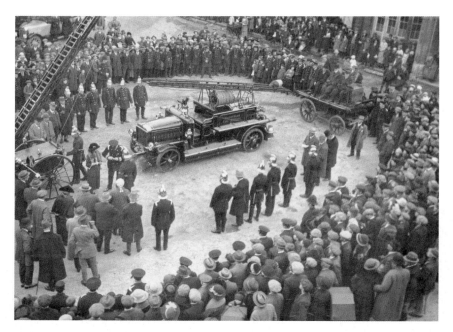

The christening of the new Leyland motor fire engine, HR 7289, in Chippenham on 21 October 1922. The town's original Merryweather manual Pump, now preserved, is seen behind the new engine. (Wiltshire Fire Brigade Museum)

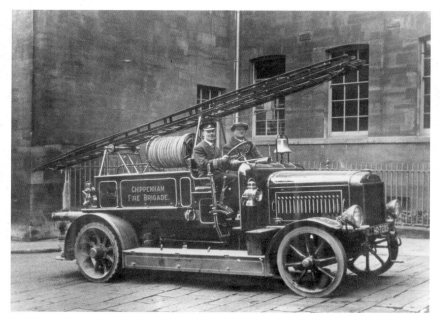

Captain Joe Buckle takes the driver's seat of Chippenham Fire Brigade's Leyland motor Pump. The 40hp engine was capable of 40–45mph, had a 400 gpm pump, 40 gallon water tank, 35ft ladder and was stowed with twenty 50ft x 2½in McGregor's 'Rob Roy' hose, all at a cost of £1,500. (Wiltshire Fire Brigade Museum)

When responding to a fire at Slade's Farm, Box, in 1929, Chippenham fireman Frederick Kidd was thrown from this appliance as it turned into Bath Road. He died instantly from a broken neck. The funeral cortege is seen passing through market place carrying the body of Fireman Kidd to the cemetery. (Chippenham Museum and Heritage Centre)

Corsham Fire Brigade's horse-drawn manual fire engine in 1899. It was known to have been in use prior to 1877 and, as a result of repairs and modifications, continued in service until 1939 when it was sold to an engineering firm in Bath for £35. (Wiltshire Fire Brigade Museum)

This 5in manual Pump was built by Samuel Phillips, *c.*1760. It served with Malmesbury Fire Brigade until replaced by a steamer in 1912. Merryweather & Sons Ltd made an offer for the manual Pump but the Fire Brigade Committee declined as they were unsure of the reliability of 'the new fangled modern appliance'. In retirement the Pump has been kept in the verger's vestry at Malmesbury Abbey but is now at the local Athelstan Museum. (Wiltshire Fire Brigade Museum)

The unveiling of Malmesbury Fire Brigade's new solid tyre Dennis motor fire engine, MR 5084 'King Athelstan', in November 1925. The 250–300 gpm light turbine engine was complete with ladder, hose-reel and 4in suction hose. The commissioning ceremony was staged outside the Cross Hayes Fire Station. (Ian Scott)

A large fire attended by Malmesbury Fire Brigade, with Dennis motor fire engine MR 5084, at Sopworth Manor. The fire was in 1929 when the manor was owned by Colonel and Lady Stanley; the damage was estimated at £25,000. (Wiltshire Fire Brigade Museum)

Malmesbury Fire Brigade also operated an ambulance service. A benefactor, Scott MacKirdy, gifted the brigade a motor ambulance which is seen here outside the fire station in 1927. (Wiltshire Fire Brigade Museum)

The horse-drawn manual fire engine used by Calne Fire Brigade during the mid- to late nineteenth century. (Wiltshire Fire Brigade Museum)

Opposite above: This Ford lorry was obtained from the Gas and Electricity Department for use by Calne Fire Brigade, *c.*1929–30. It was fitted with a manual Pump which had been converted for operation by a 5hp petrol engine in 1922 at a cost of £210. (Wiltshire Fire Brigade Museum)

Below: Pump Escape AM 2779, based on a Commer chassis, was built by Henry Simonis of Willesden, London. It was commissioned by Salisbury Fire Brigade in 1913 and christened 'The Fawcett' as a tribute to a former chief officer of the brigade. (Dennis Hill collection)

During the First World War, Salisbury Fire Brigade obtained this 30hp Beeston-Humber light motor engine, AM 3763, which had formerly been a hearse. It was converted at a cost of £145 into a Hose and Escape Tender. The two-section escape ladder was probably 30ft or 35ft, and was produced by William Rose & Co. It is known that they also supplied this type to Salisbury, Swindon New and Swindon Fire Brigades. (Wiltshire Fire Brigade Museum)

Chief Officer Hardy stands in the road as Dennis PE WV 3993 turns out from the station in Salt Lane, Salisbury, c.1936. The station, costing £1,700, opened with a civic reception on 1 May 1907 and remained in use until the current station opened in 1964. The appliance in the background is a Tilling Stevens Tender named 'Frank Baker', a light appliance without a built in-pump, which towed a trailer pump when required. It was used for chimney and small fires, and was kept in the centre bay which had no appliance room doors, so it could only turn out by moving the Pump or Pump Escape. (Jim Knowlton)

Salisbury Fire Brigade personnel with a 1930 Dennis Pump and 1933 PE outside the station in Salt Lane. The Pump was named 'The Chief' and the PE 'The Chairman'. The nameplates are seen below the windscreens. Chief Officer Hardy, the mayor and committee chairman stand in front of the Pump. This c.1936 scene marks the opening of an extension to the station which cost £3,500. (Jim Knowlton)

Dennis PE WV 3993 in attendance at a well-established fire in the Co-op, 1 Milford Street, Salisbury, in 1937. (Wiltshire Fire Brigade Museum)

Dennis PE WV 3993 and Fordson CMR 968 outside the station in Salt Lane, Salisbury, in 1958.
(The late Joe Hain)

In 1905 Mere Fire Brigade took delivery of a 250gpm Shand Mason steamer Pump. In early 1927
it was decided to mount the steamer on a lorry chassis, and subsequently a 1912 Thornycroft was
purchased second-hand from the local firm of Waltons and conversion carried out costing £57. Chief
Officer Lt G. Brice and crew pose with the motor fire engine. (Wiltshire Fire Brigade Museum)

PARCELS DEPARTMENT, _____ STATION,

Mr Capt Underwood
Fire Brigade

Dr. to THE LONDON & SOUTH WESTERN RAILWAY CO.

Waterlow & Sons Limited, Printers, Dunstable and London.

N.B.—All cheques to be drawn to the order of the L. & S. W. Ry. Co.

Date.	Where from.	No. and Description.	Weight.	Rate.	Paid on.	Cartage.	Total to Pay.
			cwts. qrs. lbs.		£ s. d.	£ s. d.	£ s. d.
18	To Newton Tony	1 Fire Engine					7 6
24		1					7 6
							15 0

AMESBURY
No. 55434 Aug 19th 191
Received from Underwood
on account of the London & South
Western Railway Co. the sum of
Fifteen Shillings

£ : 15 : 0 COLLECTOR

Any servant of the Company taking money must give such at the time of booking, and entered
The Company are not responsible for any
and paid for accordingly.
Please pay the amount above stated to the Carman, and sign his sheet, as he is not allowed to make any abatement, or to leave the goods without payment in full.
The Company deliver ordinary Parcels (which are conveyed by Passenger train) FREE within 2½ miles of Somerset House, and at the Country
stations where delivery is customary, within a mile of the Station.
It is requested that any irregularity may be notified immediately to the SUPERINTENDENT OF THE LINE, Waterloo Station.
SEE OTHER SIDE.

On 3 November 1902 Amesbury Fire Brigade paid £90 for a second-hand Shand Mason & Co. London Fire Brigade pattern 100gpm manual fire engine with equipment. Interestingly, as shown in this account for 18 August 1911, the fire engine attended a fire in Newton Tony and was taken to the incident by train from Amesbury Railway Station and returned there at a cost of 15s.

Amesbury Fire Brigade Merryweather Motor Pump No.6422, LN 4884, christened 'Antrobus' after Lord of the Manor Sir Edmund Antrobus. It was purchased c.1920 and served the town until c.1937. (Amesbury Fire Station collection)

. TROWBRIDGE FIRE BRIGADE .

A fire at the woollen mills of Samuel Salter & Co. Ltd, Court Street, Trowbridge, on 10 August 1931 resulted in severe damage to two five-storey buildings, which largely collapsed, and to the contents. The damage was estimated at £50,000. (Trowbridge Fire Station collection)

Opposite above: This Trowbridge Steamer was commissioned in 1899 and christened 'The Harry Sanders' by Mrs G. Palmer (Palmer & MacKay's owned a woollen mill in the town), who broke a bottle of champagne over it. Revd Harry Sanders was later appointed chairman of the council. At the time an archway of the market house provided temporary housing for the steamer. (Wiltshire Fire Brigade Museum)

Opposite below: Trowbridge Fire Brigade's Halley 450 gpm motor fire engine, HR 8049, was commissioned in April 1923. The cost was £1,520 and it appears here in front of the Chairman of the Council's home in Seend, where it was christened 'Vigilant' by his wife, Mrs R.C. Usher. (Wiltshire Fire Brigade Museum)

Bradford-on-Avon Fire Brigade with a manual fire engine and Shand Mason escape at the fire station, which was to the rear of the town hall, c.1885. (Wiltshire Fire Brigade Museum)

The fire escape in the previous picture, built by Shand Mason, Blackfriars, London, was possibly commissioned by the local Moulton Co. for Bradford-on-Avon UDC Fire Brigade. The company later became Spencer Moulton, which then became Avon Rubber Co. The preserved escape is seen in the drill yard of Bradford-on-Avon Fire Station, c.1981–82. (Dennis Hill)

Melksham Fire Brigade with their manual fire engine and extension ladders at Palmer & MacKay's, Court Mills, Trowbridge, in the late nineteenth century. (Wiltshire Fire Brigade Museum)

Chief Officer Captain A. Dewey with his officers and men of Warminster UDC Fire Brigade and their Dennis Pump, WV 9807, c.1937. The picture was taken in The Close, opposite the fire station which the brigade occupied from 1905–66. (Warminster Fire Station collection)

Devizes Fire Brigade in 1905 at the station which was behind The Shambles market hall (seen in the background). The horse-drawn Pump also served to carry crews to fires. The hand cart contains a rolled canvas hose and, to the rear, a cart carries a leather hose rolled on a drum. The fire escape behind the Pump was presented to the town in 1873 by the Royal Society for Protection of Life from Fire. (Wiltshire Fire Brigade Museum)

Lake Fire Brigade's Albion/Merryweather appliance which was fitted with a 400/500 gpm three cylinder reciprocating pump, with large air cylinder visible at the rear. The appliance was probably commissioned in 1935–36 and this picture taken a couple of years later. Lake had lost their previous manual fire engine when the fire station burnt down in 1932. It is surprising that Lake, a

hamlet, should have such a grand appliance. However, Lake House is a large property which, at the time, was owned by Lady Janet Bailey, daughter of the shipping magnet Lord Inchape. Lake House had been virtually destroyed by fire on Good Friday 1912 so the Bailey family possibly paid for the new appliance. (Wiltshire Fire Brigade Museum)

two

Auxiliary Fire Service and National Fire Service

A fire tender in use by the War Department's Hawthorn Fire Section at Box in 1940. This was an area of Wiltshire with numerous military underground storage facilities. (Wiltshire Fire Brigade Museum)

Opposite: Market Lavington Fire Brigade obtained a steamer Pump in 1924 and, five years later, local motor engineer Reg Milsom mounted the pump on the chassis of a bus bought from Bristol Tramways for £25. Village verger Tom Merritt is the brigade captain with his crew, which included his two sons, in this early Second World War scene. (Wiltshire Fire Brigade Museum)

Dennis Pump Ladder WV 1627 believed to be travelling along Milton Road, Swindon, towards the old Medical Fund Hospital, c.early 1941. Chief Officer Roy Howells is thought to be the officer-in-charge of the appliance and Fireman Bert Read is standing offside, third back. The appliance to the rear is a Home Office issue Heavy Unit based on a Morris commercial chassis. These were supplied for use by the AFS and a cipher on the driver's door, GV1R, reflected its Home Office origin. (John Read)

Dennis Pump Escape MW 3317 was purchased for Devizes Fire Brigade in November 1928 at £1,675. It had an output of 500/700 gpm and a 50ft Ajax escape ladder. Here it is carrying out a deep-lift test at Rotherstone Bridge on the Kennet and Avon Canal, Devizes, c.1940. Note the headlamp covers, white painted mudguards and the deletion of 'Devizes' on the body panel to comply with wartime regulations. (Wiltshire Fire Brigade Museum)

Wroughton NFS personnel outside Millbrook House, whose stables were used as the fire station. The Humber saloon was donated by Mrs Arnold-Forster of Basset Down and was modified with ladder gantries and a towing hitch for the 200 gpm Coventry Climax Trailer Pump, which was powered by a Jowett air-cooled two-cylinder engine. (Wroughton History Group)

Fireman Arthur Tovey on watch room duty at NFS Station 39-A-1-X, Devizes Road, Swindon, in 1943. (Arthur and Monica Tovey)

NFS personnel relaxing at Station 39-A-1-X, Devizes Road, Swindon, c.1941–42. In these early days of the NFS, various vehicles were pressed into service, as can be seen by the type in use here. (Arthur and Monica Tovey)

NFS canteen van in Swindon operated by Molly Padget on the left and an unknown colleague, c.1943.
(Arthur and Monica Tovey)

Swindon NFS personnel taking part in the 'Salute The Soldier' week in Old Town during April 1944.
Events such as these were staged throughout the country to raise money for the war effort. (Arthur and
Monica Tovey)

Chippenham NFS crew, from left to right: E. Milsom, F. Roscoe, W. Vaughan, I. Haines, G. Hazell and F. Freeguard and their Second World War trailer pump. This crew attended incidents during the Blitz in Bristol, Avonmouth, Coventry and Birmingham. (Chippenham Museum & Heritage Centre)

Under the terms of the Fire Brigades Act 1938, Mere & Tisbury RDC provided this Dennis 'New World' Appliance for Tisbury Fire Brigade in 1939. Mere Fire Brigade had an identical appliance and both brigades also received 350/500 gpm Trailer Pumps. With this appliance crews from Tisbury attended calls in Southampton and Gosport during the wartime Blitz. This appliance survives in preservation with a former Salisbury fireman. (Wiltshire Fire Brigade Museum)

The Dennis 350 gpm Pump was purchased new by Amesbury Rural District Council, *c.*1937. The officers, T. Mathews, A. Sloan and C.A. Eyres, are pictured in 1942 with their crews who attended calls during the Blitz of 1941 and 1942 in London, Reading, Gosport, Bath, Bristol and Avonmouth. (Amesbury Fire Station collection)

An American Army officer takes the salute as Ludgershall NFS personnel march past, possibly on a parade in 1945 to mark the end of the war. (Wiltshire Fire Brigade Museum)

Leyland FK8A Pump Escape CMW 356 was delivered new to Trowbridge UDC Fire Brigade in June 1940 and replaced the 1923 Halley Pump. The 85bhp Leyland had a 500/700 gpm output and came complete with a hose reel, Francis electric bell, searchlight and 50ft escape ladder at a cost of £1,700. It is seen here during its NFS years. (Wiltshire Fire Brigade Museum)

An NFS crew carrying out a demonstration with their Fordson Pump at the County Ground, Swindon, in 1944. (Arthur and Monica Tovey)

An AFS crew at the Salisbury Pump Competitions in 1950 with an ex-NFS Bedford Heavy Unit FYH 407. (Arthur and Monica Tovey)

An AFS crew lowering a light portable pump onto a Bikini raft, using a vehicle-mounted crane, at Bowood Park on 6 August 1960. (Arthur & Monica Tovey)

Chippenham Fire Station's Green Goddess NYR 26 being prepared with a bivouac for overnight sleeping during an AFS exercise at Erlestoke on 28 October 1960. (Wiltshire Fire Brigade Museum)

Swindon AFS contingent at Swindon Fire Station prior to exercise 'Corn Cob' in Exeter on 21–23 April 1961. From left to right: Commer Superpoise General-Purpose Lorry, Bedford Green Goddess Pump and two Land Rovers with twin orange flashing lights on the bonnet. (Arthur and Monica Tovey)

AFS appliances assembled at Swindon Fire Station prior to weekend exercise 'Four Shires' at the Fire Service Training Centre, Moreton-in-March on 9 March 1963. (Arthur and Monica Tovey)

AFS Control Unit and Dispatch Riders on exercise at the Army School of Civil Defence, Devizes, on 24 November 1963. (Arthur and Monica Tovey)

AFS crew getting to work with light portable pumps from a portable dam at the Army School of Civil Defence, Devizes, on 24 November 1963. (Arthur and Monica Tovey)

Firewomen of the AFS laying a field telephone cable at the Army School of Civil Defence, Devizes, on 24 November 1963. (Arthur and Monica Tovey)

An AFS crew at drill with a Green Goddess 4x2, working from a portable dam in the drill yard at Swindon Fire Station, c.1965. (Arthur and Monica Tovey)

Monica Tovey and Olive Ashley of Swindon AFS in a Control Unit leading a convoy of Green Goddesses to Charmouth, Devon. (Arthur & Monica Tovey)

Monica Tovey with Green Goddess 4X2 EP NYR 551 at Swindon Fire Station in early 1968, prior to the disbandment of the AFS. (Arthur and Monica Tovey)

The Stand–Down Parade at Trowbridge Fire Station on 27 April 1968 following the Government's decision that the services provided by the AFS and the Civil Defence were no longer necessary. (Arthur and Monica Tovey)

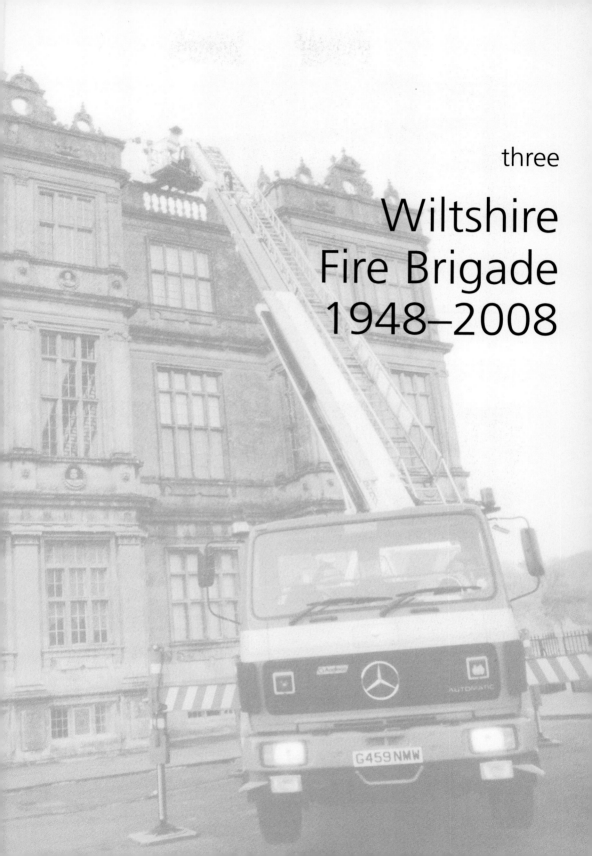

three

Wiltshire
Fire Brigade
1948–2008

This shows the station and headquarters of Swindon Fire Brigade in Cromwell Street. When the brigade first occupied the premises in 1899 it was intended to be temporary, but it was not until 1959 that Wiltshire Fire Brigade moved into the new station in Drove Road. (Matt Jackson collection)

Leyland Cub FKT2 Pump Escape CHR 598 was delivered new to Swindon Municipal Borough in November 1939. It served at Cromwell Street station but had been transferred to Amesbury as a Pump Ladder before the Drove Road station was opened. On preservation it has been returned to its original PE format. (Dennis Hill)

The appliance room at Swindon's Drove Road station following occupancy in 1959. From left to right: Fordson EST which could tow a Dennis Trailer Pump, Austin Merryweather 60ft TL GXN 217 with power extension and a Barton front drive Pump (which was primed through the engine carburettor; it was withdrawn from service in 1960), Commer/Miles WrT/E SWV 297 with Bailey extra heavy escape, Commer/Miles WrT KMR 388 and Commer/Whitsun WrT GMW 953. (John Gentleman)

The new five-bay Swindon Fire Station in Drove Road which opened in 1959. Today it is on the south side of Swindon's infamous 'Magic Roundabout' road system and opposite Swindon Town Football Club. (Wiltshire Fire Brigade Museum)

The 1960 Bedford STL with 100ft Magirus ladder WWV 439 during an HMI Inspection at Swindon Fire Station. This appliance, costing £8,900, replaced the Austin Merryweather 60ft TL GXN 217. (Wiltshire Fire Brigade Museum)

Fire scene at John Webb (Swindon) Ltd, Builders Merchants, Station Road, Swindon, on 18 October 1967. The attendance for this incident was six Pumps, TL, ET and AFS EP. (Arthur and Monica Tovey)

A fire at the Bell Hotel, High Street, Old Town, Swindon, was attended by four Pumps and a TL. When new in 1972, the Bedford TK HCB-Angus WWV 947K served at Chippenham before being transferred to Cricklade. (Wiltshire Newspapers)

Opposite above: Swindon's Bedford TL WWV 439 in operation as a water tower during the fire at John Webb (Swindon) Ltd, Station Road, Swindon, on 18 October 1967 (Arthur and Monica Tovey collection)

Opposite below: Leyland Comet WrT HMW 291 at Swindon Station in 1966. The chassis for this appliance was one of fifty ordered by the Ministry of Works and Buildings in 1950 to fulfil a shortage of fire engine chassis after the Second World War. The chassis left the Leyland Works in October 1951 with the bodywork completed by a company named Windover. HMW 291 ended its days in a Devizes scrap yard. (Ian Scott)

1951 Dennis F12 HMR 765 and Dennis WrLR RMW 21Y at Swindon Station. Wiltshire Fire Brigade purchased RMW 21Y and RMW 22Y in 1983 and these were allocated to Swindon and Stratton Stations respectively. They were the first Dennis appliances in the brigade since the F12 was obtained in1951. (John Gentleman collection)

1951 Dennis F12 PE HMR 765 at Swindon Station. This appliance was stationed at Salisbury and had operated as a PL at the time when it was withdrawn in 1978. It is now preserved by Wiltshire Fire and Rescue Service. In appearance the coach-built Dennis F12 was surely the classiest fire appliance of all time. With its Rolls-Royce straight eight-cylinder engine it was a satisfying experience to drive on a 'shout'. On a two-Pump turnout with a Bedford TK, the latter was just a speck in the rear view mirror of the Dennis. (Wiltshire Fire Brigade)

'Fire Fighting in Wiltshire through the Ages' was the theme of this publicity shoot, c.1985. A manual, steamer and modern Dennis WrL/R RMW 21Y line up at the former Second World War RAF Wroughton airfield. (Wiltshire Fire Brigade)

For its entire service the 1974 Dodge K850/Perkins Merryweather PMR 713M was based at Swindon Fire Station as an Emergency Tender until disposal. (Dave Carter collection)

1974 Dodge K850/Perkins Merryweather GHR 618N was initially based at Salisbury as an Emergency Tender before moving to Westbury as a Damage Control Unit. Later it was moved to Swindon where it continued in the same role until disposal. (Dave Carter collection)

1972 Dodge K850/Perkins HCB–Angus CMW 687L WrL/R based at Ramsbury Fire Station after transfer from Swindon. (Dave Carter collection)

1995 ERF EC8 Prime Mover N170 KAM based at Stratton with a Damage Contol Unit pod. (Dave Carter collection)

An ATV, Leyland Cub FK6 Pump Escape AAM 695 and Commer WrT JHR 171 at the Second World War-built fire station in Dallas Road, Chippenham, which was adopted by Wiltshire Fire Brigade on 1 April 1948. The current fire station stands on the same site and during construction a temporary site in Cocklebury Road was used. (Graham Taylor)

A fire at Littlefield, one of Marlborough College's residential houses, on 11 April 1962. ACFO C.J. Sanders was in charge of the incident which was attended by six Pumps from Marlborough, Ramsbury, Pewsey and Swindon plus Salvage Tender and TL from Swindon, which is seen here preparing to get to work. (Arthur and Monica Tovey)

Leyland Cub FK6 PE AAM 695 was delivered new to Chippenham Fire Brigade in May 1936. (Graham Taylor)

On 17 August 1973 Chippenham's Range Rover ET and Swindon's Dodge ET attended this serious crash on the M4 westbound between Junctions 16 and 17, involving a National Express coach *(top)* and a flatbed lorry *(bottom)*. DO Mike Tatem was officer-in-charge of the incident, at which there were a number of fatalities, and it was necessary to close the motorway in both directions. In the early 1980s there were a number of coach crashes in the country and subsequent legislation was introduced requiring seat belts to be fitted in coaches. (Wiltshire Fire Brigade)

1976 Range Rover Carmichael KMR 673P Emergency Tender based at Chippenham. This was an appliance designed by the Brigade's Technical Committee to meet the needs of emergencies on the M4 motorway which passes east to west through the county. (Dave Carter collection)

1982 Dodge GO9/Perkins Benson NAM 362X Control Unit/Canteen Van based at Chippenham but seen here at Amesbury Abbey. This appliance was a considerable improvement on the L4Vs which previously arrived at the fire-ground with tea urns and a tray of sandwiches. (Wiltshire Fire Brigade Museum)

2002 Mercedes Econic WU02 KLK Emergency Support Unit based at Chippenham. (Dave Carter collection)

Former Chippenham Bedford TK HCB-Angus SMW 659J WrL at Brigade Workshops, Trowbridge, awaiting disposal in September 1985.

Bedford TK HCB–Angus WWV 947K WrL being loaded into a Hercules during a snow storm at RAF Lyneham in early 1987. The appliance was a donation destined for Banjul in the Republic of Gambia. (John Lakey)

1979 Dodge K113/Perkins CFE UMW 329T at Calne Station where it served until disposal. (Dave Carter collection)

Bedford TK BHR 369B WrT and Austin CHR 514 ET at the four-bay Salisbury Fire Station, which opened in 1964. (Wiltshire Fire Brigade Museum)

1940 Leyland Merryweather GHW 415 TL, which served at Salisbury for twenty years from 1 April 1948. Prior to this the appliance was with the NFS in Bristol, and currently survives in preservation.

AEC Mercury Merryweather MMR 217G TL replaced the Leyland TL at Salisbury, where it was based for its entire service with the brigade. (David Carter collection)

Dodge G16 E555 XMR Prime Mover with Foam Unit pod at Salisbury. The appliance was later transferred to Devizes, where it was based until disposal. (Dave Carter collection)

Salisbury's Mercedes-Bronto Skylift G459 NMW Hydraulic Platform at work on the roof of Lord Bath's Longleat House. (Dave Carter collection)

Salisbury Station with a line-up of appliances. From left to right: Dennis Sabre WrL/R, Mercedes Compact Pump, Mercedes–Bronto Skylift, Mercedes-Econic Emergency Support Unit and Dodge G16 Prime Mover with Incident Control pod. (Dave Carter collection)

The old and the new Aerial Platforms at Salisbury with Mercedes–Bronto G459 NMW and Mercedes-Econic WU54 EKA. (Dave Carter collection)

1980 Leyland XYA 369W Water Carrier based at Wilton Fire Station. A number of these ex-milk tankers were purchased by the brigade to assist with supplies for fire fighting in rural areas and for water ferrying at protracted incidents.(Dave Carter collection)

Leyland Cub FKT2 Pump at Amesbury Fire Station in 1965. The appliance had previously served as a Pump Escape at Swindon. (Ian Scott)

Commer/Whitson GMW 526 Water Tender was based at Amesbury until disposal and is seen here in preservation at Bishops Lydeard near Taunton on 4 August 1996. (Dennis Hill)

Bedford TK HCB-Angus PHR 591H Water Tender Ladder in the drill yard at Amesbury, *c*.1975. This appliance had previously served at Salisbury and became a brigade spare after leaving Amesbury. (Maurice Cole)

Amesbury's Dodge WrL/R at The Maltings in Salisbury, the morning after fire destroyed the roofs of the then-new shopping complex. (Amesbury Fire Station collection)

Four-gallon Jerry cans being removed by Amesbury and Tidworth Army Fire Service personnel following a fire in a Stalwart amphibious high mobility load carrier at the junction of Beacon Hill (A303) and Marlborough Road in 1970. Fires in loads carried by this type of army vehicle were not unknown as the exhaust pipes were positioned vertically at the rear of the cabs. It would seem strange then that one should be used for transporting fuel cans. The fire appliance seen is a Bedford Pump of the Army Fire Service. (Amesbury Fire Station collection)

Right: Dodge HCB–Angus WrL/R MHR 849X and MHR 850X at Amesbury Abbey in 1982 prior to allocation to Chippenham and Amesbury Stations. MHR 849X also served at Ludgershall until disposal. (Wiltshire Fire Brigade)

Below: 1978 Dodge WrL/R SAM 186S in the drill yard at Pewsey. This appliance had previously served at Amesbury and later was transferred from Pewsey to Bradford-on-Avon. (Wiltshire Fire Brigade Museum)

Dodge HCB-Angus D688 RMR WrL/R was allocated to Pewsey in 1987 where it served until disposal. (Dave Carter collection)

Ex-Fire Service College, Moreton-in-Marsh Dennis F12 GYR 879 was adopted by Wiltshire Fire Brigade pending donation to a proposed National Fire Brigade Museum. The appliance is seen here on 29 June 1987 at Pewsey Fire Station whose personnel had volunteered to carry out renovation.

Commer/Miles Pump Escape PWV 774 in the drill yard at Trowbridge Fire Station where it was based until disposal. (Ian Scott)

1980 Dodge G1313-100 Cheshire Fire Engineering GMW 182W WrL/R based at Trowbridge and seen here in the station drill yard in September 1985.

2002 Mercedes-Econic WV52 CGG Emergency Support Unit and 2002 Dennis Sabre WV52 CGU WrL/R under the covered wash at Trowbridge. The Dennis was subsequently transferred to Malmesbury. (Dave Carter collection)

2004 Mercedes-Econic WX53 FBG Hydraulic Platform allocated to Swindon and seen here at Trowbridge Fire Station. (Dave Carter collection)

2006 Ford WX56 VZP X-Ray Unit outside the workshops at Trowbridge Fire Station. This vehicle, based at Westbury, is used at off-road incidents where access for major appliances would be a problem. (Dave Carter collection)

1980 Dodge S56 Carmichael FHR 622W ET, based at Trowbridge, stands here on the station forecourt. (Dave Carter collection)

2004 MAN DG53 FYV Incident Response Unit based at Melksham. The Government have provided a number of these vehicles to fire brigades around the country for use at major incidents. They carry a range of equipment suitable for use at various types of emergency. (Dave Carter collection)

Dennis Sabres at Warminster Fire Station: WU54 EJX WrL/R, R102 HMW WrL/R and N421 MAM WrL. The appliance in the centre was originally based at Swindon and is now with Cooper Tyres in Melksham. (Dave Carter collection)

A 1997 Ford Iveco Cargo Prime Mover R103 HMW with Chemical Incident Unit pod based at Warminster. (Dave Carter collection)

The worst fire in Warminster since 1920 occurred on 21 December 2000 when, at around 08:00 hours, flames engulfed the roof of Balfour News, a Grade II listed building in the market place. The fire, which spread to adjoining terraced properties, was attended by appliances from Warminster, Westbury, Trowbridge, Calne, Amesbury, Tisbury, Melksham, Devizes, Corsham, Ludgershall, Cooper Tyres Melksham and from Avon and Somerset Fire and Rescue Services. (Warminster Fire Station collection)

A Commer/Miles HMW 347 WrT based at Devizes Fire Station with an unknown Commer at the rear. The two vehicles are parked by The Green in Devizes, c.1969. (Ian Scott)

Devizes personnel with Dennis Pump Escape outside the fire station in Estcourt Street shortly after the formation of Wiltshire Fire Brigade. (Wiltshire Fire Brigade Museum)

One of the early Bedford TK Water Tenders 446 DHR, which was based at Devizes and appears in the station yard. (Dave Carter collection)

A Bedford TK GHR 843D Foam Carrier allocated to Devizes Fire Station, where it is seen in the drill yard. (Dave Carter collection)

These appliances are lined-up in Caen Hill, Devizes, *(top)* where a ten-Pump attendance was required for a fire in J. Jones car breakers yard on 7 July 2005 *(bottom)*. (Dave Carter collection)

An Austin K2 ATV GXH 372 and trailer pump of the former Market Lavington Fire Brigade outside the village station, following adoption by the Wiltshire Fire Authority. At this time the station, together with those of Box, Aldbourne and Ramsbury, were referred to as Local Light Units. Market Lavington Station closed in 1953 but the Austin ATV survived until disposal in 1966. (Wiltshire Fire Brigade Museum)

In 1985 Chief Fire Officer Dennis Robins opened a new Brigade Training Centre on the former Hopton Barracks army camp in Devizes. A Dodge Carmichael KMW 890P WrL was allocated to the Training Centre and is seen here in September 1985. This appliance had previously been operational at Stratton.

Ex-Auxiliary Fire Service Bedford 372 ALC Breakdown Lorry based at Brigade Workshops, Trowbridge Fire Station. (Dave Carter collection)

Wiltshire Fire Brigade's first five Dennis Sabre WrL/R appliances taking a photo call at The National Trust's Heywood House near Westbury in 1995. (Wiltshire Fire Brigade)

The Brigade Museum Collection housed in the former stable block of Wiltshire Fire and Rescue Service Headquarters, Manor House, Potterne.

Thatched properties are commonplace in Wiltshire and incidents involving them are regular features. This 1937 fire at the thatched Cross Keys Public House in Rowde resulted in severe damage, the cost of which was £3,000. The property was rebuilt, but today the roof is no longer covered by thatch. (Wiltshire Fire Brigade Museum)

On 20 February 1974 the 09.43 hours Fawley to Tiverton freight train carrying 128,000 gallons of fuel derailed on the south side of Westbury Railway Station. Eight Esso tank wagons carrying kerosene turned on their sides and three more were derailed but stayed upright, as did five petrol tank wagons. Five Pumps were mobilised to the incident at 12.55 hours and the railway station was closed whilst foam was used to cover the leaking wagons. Had the petrol wagons turned over and leaked their contents, the incident could have been far worse. (Warminster Fire Station collection)

Opposite above: Fire severely damaged one of Wiltshire's stately homes, Spye Park near Bromham, on 8 August 1974. 10/12 Pumps from around the county were mobilised for firefighting, water-relaying and salvage. The hydraulic platform from Swindon was being evaluated by the brigade at the time. Although the building could not be saved, valuable salvage work was achieved at this fire, the cause of which was the flame from a blowtorch. Spye Park had frequently been a retreat for the Queen Mother. (Graham Taylor collection)

Opposite below: This RTA occurred on the A4 at Corsham on 7 May 1975, when this Bristol Lodekka bus, making a return trip from Calne to Bath, struck a fallen tree. Driver Ray Cormack was killed in the accident, which was attended by Corsham and Chippenham fire crews. (Graham Taylor collection)

One of the fires involving property in Marlborough Town Centre was this fire discovered by an off-duty fireman at 17.26 hours on 8 June 1998. The fire started in Halls Butchers shop in High Street and the attendance built up to fifteen Pumps and a Hydraulic Platform from Swindon. Firefighting operations were led by DCFO Neil Wright (Wiltshire Fire Brigade)

Opposite above and below: Barn fires in Wiltshire, as with other rural brigades, are a common occurrence. The causes vary from a hot vehicle exhaust to carelessly discarded smoking material and, all too often, as a result of arson. LFm Bob Hill and a fellow Devizes fireman and a crew from Calne can only hope to prevent a spread to adjoining property. (Wiltshire Fire Brigade)

An incident at The
Maltings shopping
complex in Salisbury
at which this young
policeman was prepared
to help the firefighters
with their hose supplies.
(Wiltshire Fire Brigade)

Scania HP K629 OAM at an office block in Swindon. This appliance appears in the Marlborough fire
photograph on the previous page. (Wiltshire Fire Brigade)

Wiltshire Fire Brigade received a 999 call at 02:34 hours on 3 January 1992, reporting a fire in an aircraft hangar at RAF Hullavington, an airfield built between the wars. The 'C' Type hangar was used for parachute packing and storage. Despite a large attendance, including appliances from surrounding brigades, the fact that the contents were in a large, undivided area contributed significantly to the destruction of the building. The fire had been started deliberately and the arsonists were later charged. (Wiltshire Fire Brigade)

Fire at Dible and Roy furniture shop in High Street, Marlborough, on 9 October 1975. The fire, which was attended by ten Pumps and a TL, was started by a firework. The property was extensively damaged and the neighbouring properties also suffered various degrees of damage. (Wiltshire Fire Brigade)

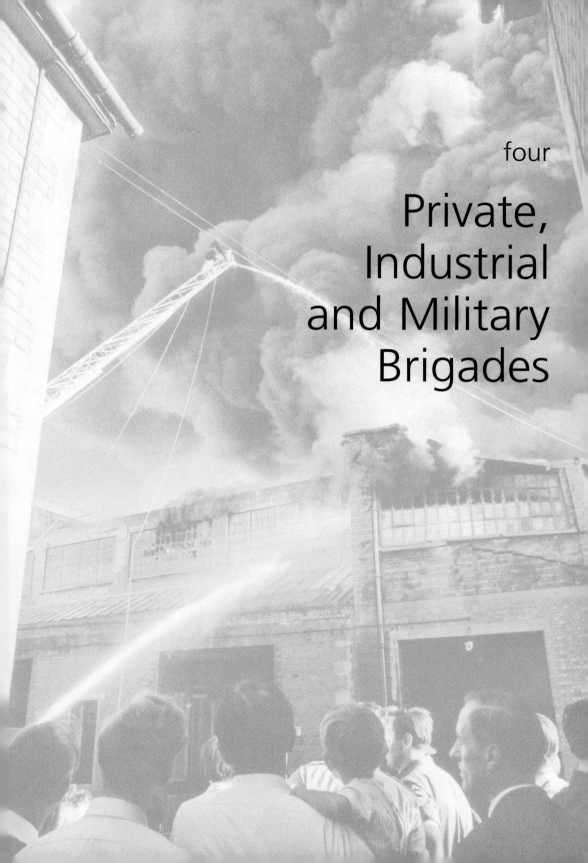

four

Private,
Industrial
and Military
Brigades

R.A. Lister, the world-renowned manufacturer of stationary engines, had a factory in North Wroughton from 1946. The company fire section is seen here in 1978 with their fire appliance, which consisted of a later version of an auto-truck propelled by a Lister twin cylinder diesel engine. (Wroughton History Group)

Opposite above: Lord Longford with his Castle Estate Fire Brigade after the inauguration of a mains water supply in 1902. The castle was served by a 4in ring main with six hydrants. This was fed by a 6in main from a 50,000 gallon hilltop reservoir. It appears the mains pressure was such that it could supply four jets capable of reaching the top of the castle. (Wiltshire Fire Brigade Museum)

Opposite below: Longford Castle Estate Fire Brigade with a Simonis Motor Fire Engine at the Cottage Garden Show, Longford Castle, Odstock, in 1913. (Wiltshire Fire Brigade Museum)

Ushers Brewery Fire Brigade, Trowbridge, had an establishment of two officers and twelve men in 1936, all of whom were brewery employees paid a retaining fee for fire duties. The brigade had a 250 gpm Dennis Pump and a Morris motor tender with ladder. The Ushers Pump also responded to fire calls in the town. (Wiltshire Fire Brigade Museum)

Saxby & Farmer Ltd Works Fire Brigade with hand-drawn manual fire engine at the engineering works in Chippenham, *c.*1905. A monogram on the side of the hand-cart displayed the letters 'EOD', which stood for Evans O'Donnell & Co. Ltd, formed as an engineering company alongside the Paddington–Bristol railway line in 1894. In 1921 Westinghouse Brake & Saxby Signal Co. Ltd. was formed on this site. (Chippenham Museum & Heritage Centre)

The Westinghouse Brake & Signal Co. Ltd Works Fire Brigade responding on exercise with an ex-NFS 30hp Fordson 7V Pump Ladder in 1952. The chief officer at the time was A.V. Thomas, former Wiltshire Fire Brigade Chief Fire Officer. (Chippenham Museum & Heritage Centre)

Westinghouse replaced their wartime Fordson appliance, with this Dennis F8 OMR 818 Pump Ladder and trailer pump, which was still operational in the 1970s but is seen here in preservation. (Wiltshire Fire Brigade Museum)

The engineering works of the Westinghouse Brake & Signal Co. Ltd were severely damaged by this fire on the premises in 1987. (Wiltshire Fire Brigade)

Dennis F8 JMW 424 served with Wiltshire Fire Brigade at Malmesbury Fire Station until disposal. It was bought by Pains–Wessex for use at their firework factory at High Post. It is seen here in preservation. (Dave Carter collection)

1926 30cwt Dennis Pump WV 6060 was supplied new to Avon India Rubber Co. Ltd in August 1934 at a cost of £667 5s. It came with 'Avon' tyres, three 8ft x 3½in suction hose, 1,000ft of delivery hose and a 30ft ladder. The Pump was used at a Southampton Docks fire during the Blitz. It was sold at auction in 1986 for £8,100 and is seen in preservation. (The late Roger Pennington)

This Bedford Pump DNX 958 was originally operated by The Rover Car Company in Solihull and subsequently by Avon Rubber Company in Melksham, possibly in the 1950s. (Cooper Tyres)

On Monday 15 August 1966 a fire broke out in the Finished Goods Store of the Avon Rubber Company in Melksham. The fire spread within the works and to nearby houses in Scotland Road. The damage was estimated at £750,000. (Cooper Tyres)

The walls of the Finished Goods Store in Scotland Road shortly before collapsing in. The fire was attended by seventy firefighters with 10/12 Pumps and a TL from Bath City Fire Brigade. (Cooper Tyres)

Austin Gypsy YWV 702 with a front-mounted pump was used by the Avon Rubber Works Fire Brigade until it was retired and loaned to 'Blazes', a fire brigade museum collection at Sandhill Park near Taunton. The museum has since closed and the whereabouts of this appliance is now unknown. (Cooper Tyres)

1983 Dodge G1313 Perkins Carmichael BDG 40Y is an ex-Gloucestershire Fire and Rescue Service WrT, operating at Cheltenham Fire Station until bought by the Avon Rubber Company. (Dave Carter collection)

A Water Rescue Unit operated by Cooper Tyres, Melksham. Mercedes G464 NMW was originally an Emergency Support Unit at Salisbury Fire Station. (Dave Carter collection)

Cooper Tyres of Melksham is affiliated to Wiltshire Fire and Rescue Service as Station 4/7 and has a compliment of sixteen operational personnel. The three former brigade appliances on the run in August 2007 are, from left to right: 1990 Mercedes Mountain Range 4x4 Water Rescue Unit G464 NMW, with a rescue inflatable boat and trailer, 1997 Dennis Sabre 500 gpm WrL/R R102 HMW ex- Swindon, and 1990 Mercedes Mountain Range Compact Pump G463 NMW ex-Warminster. The Utility Vehicle is a Mitsubishi L200 4x4 WV04 KYP.

A number of apparently Great Western Railway staff beside one of the two horse-drawn Merryweather steam fire Pumps used by the Swindon Railway Works Fire Brigade. (David Hyde collection)

Personnel of the GWR Fire Brigade Swindon with the other horse-drawn steam fire Pump in 1901. (David Hyde collection)

GWR Fire Brigade Swindon 1912 Dennis 60hp motor fire engine AM 2747, which is thought to have been the first motor fire engine in the country. The appliance was built to pass through the low tunnels in the Swindon Works and it had a steering lock which allowed it to turn in tight areas. It appears here outside the Works Fire Station. (David Hyde collection)

The smaller oil-fired Merryweather steam Pump could be towed by the Dennis motor fire engine or pulled manually. In this crew photograph, taken on 24 November 1915, the registration number of the Dennis appears in a different place on the vehicle than in the previous photograph. (David Hyde collection)

Motor fire engine outside the fire station, GWR Fire Brigade, Swindon. (David Hyde Collection)

The Pump operator working the GWR Dennis motor Pump in Bristol Street, Swindon. The first large fire at which this Pump was used was in 1915 at the Southern Laundry next to the Great Western Hotel. The last major fire it was used at was in 1942 following an air attack on the large gas holder at Swindon Railway Works. The Pump is preserved at the National Railway Museum in York. (David Hyde collection)

Water was pumped from Kemble to supply this 41,000-gallon water tank at Swindon Railway Works. It was sited in the yard by the fire station and next to it was a timber hose-drying tower used by the GWR works brigade. A finial from a line-side signal can be seen on top of the hose tower. (David Hyde collection)

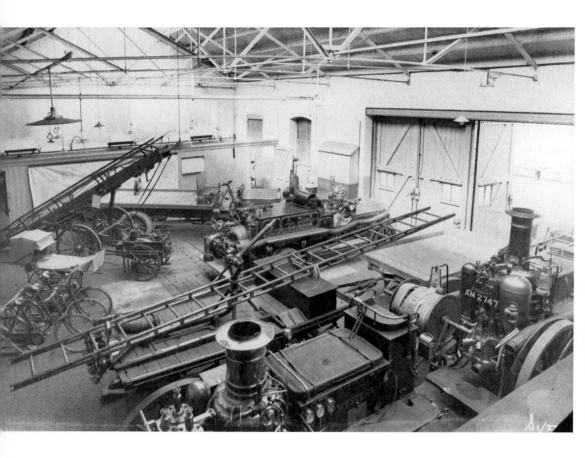

GWR Swindon Bristol Street Fire Station on 25 July 1916. In the foreground are two steam fire Pumps, the larger displaying the registration number of the Dennis motor fire engine. Between the Dennis and the steamers is a flatbed lorry towing a trailer with a ladder. The trailer appears to have hose connections at the rear. Another similar lorry at the far end of the station was used for carrying equipment. (David Hyde collection)

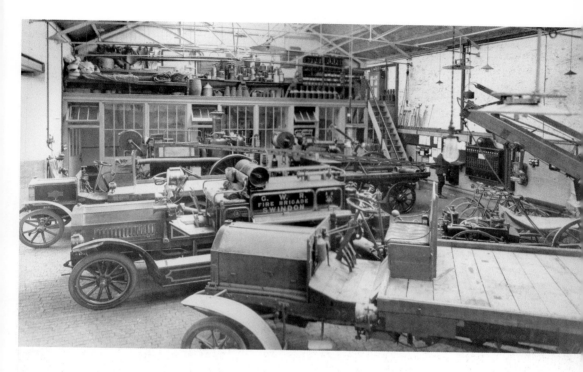

The fire station viewed from the opposite end of the building, and showing on the right-hand side wall is the call-board used to alert off-duty firemen. This operated via links to bells which were installed in their houses in the nearby railway village (David Hyde collection)

The GWR were completely self-sufficient, including the production and maintenance of fire-fighting equipment needed throughout their area of operation. Shown is the Platelayers Shop at Swindon Works on 24 April 1928, where work was being carried out on fire equipment. (David Hyde collection)

During the Second World War the Great Western Railway converted rolling stock for use as fire trains. One of those seen here in January 1941 is a Covered Carriage Truck 'Python A', No.560, with specially widened side door. (David Hyde collection)

A trailer pump was carried inside which could be swung out of the widened door and lowered from the truck using the pulley and jib on the side. (David Hyde collection)

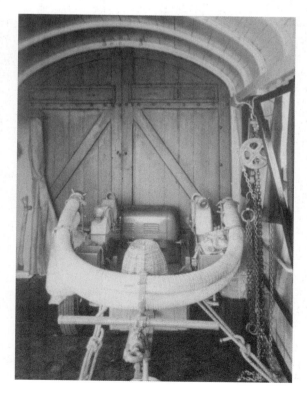

The make up of a fire train included accommodation and facilities for the firemen and is provided in this case by a converted slip coach. (David Hyde collection)

This trolley-mounted canister and scoop is a piece of fire fighting apparatus made by the GWR at the Swindon Works. This particular apparatus contained a dry powder mixture of sodium bicarbonate and calcium carbonate. (David Hyde collection)

British Railways purchased this 1942 4-cylinder 60bhp Dennis GLA 169 to replace the 1912 GWR Dennis. The new appliance had a semi-limousine body, and seating arranged transversely to accommodate a 6/7 man crew. It was originally finished in battleship grey but later re-sprayed red. It was equipped with a 500/600 gpm multi-stage turbine pump. It is seen here in the Bristol Street Fire Station. This appliance is preserved at the Science Museum at Wroughton. (David Hyde collection)

Inside British Railway's Swindon Fire Station is Land Rover PWV 230 which replaced the 1942 Dennis. The trailer pumps are two of four purchased in early 1939 for war use at the works. On the wall are the Kemble water pipeline pressure gauges and test tap. (David Hyde collection)

Royal Navy Green Goddess Emergency Pump PGW 81 responding to the Navy's first call in Wiltshire during the 1977 Firemen's Strike. The incident was a car fire at the junction of the A345 and Old Castle Road on 14 November 1977.

Opposite above: The pilot of the Bomber Command Communications Flight Avro Anson thought he was landing at RAF Old Sarum airfield on 31 July 1957, but mistakenly landed in nearby Hudson's Field recreation ground. The aircraft ended its landing run in Stratford Road. The fire appliance attending is a Thornycroft Mk 5 RAF Crash Tender from Old Sarum airfield. (Salisbury Journal)

Opposite below: Maintenance of fire-fighting equipment continued under British Railways and this was carried out in the maintenance workshop attached to the fire station. This 1980s photo shows the north end of the railway workshop, at the far side of which the track enters Swindon station. (David Hyde collection)

A scene at RAF Lyneham shortly after the invasion of the Falklands on 2 April 1982. Over the following two months Hercules transport aircraft were fitted with air-to-air refuelling equipment, seen above the cockpit of 195. The Hercules is attended by two Mk 9 Thornycroft Foam Tenders and a Land Rover TacR II Crash Rescue Truck. (Malcolm Petch)

Opposite below: 1990 Dennis HCB-Angus WrL E753 HRV with its replacement, 1998 Volvo FL6 14 Intercooler WrL G180 UPO of Serco Fire and Rescue Service. Both appliances, fitted with 2250 lpm Godiva pumps, are ex-Hampshire Fire and Rescue Service and are seen at dstl Porton Down in August 2007.

RAF Thornycroft Nubian Major Mk 9 Foam Tender 30 AG 89 at RAF Lyneham, *c.*1982. (Malcolm Petch)

RAF Land Rover HCB-Angus TacR II and Crash Rescue Truck 31 AG 58 at RAF Lyneham, *c.*1982.
(Malcolm Petch)

RAF Lyneham has two fire sections. 2 Group TAC AC is manned by RAF personnel and provides fire cover for aircraft movements away from Lyneham. The Defence Fire and Rescue Service covers emergencies on the airfield site. Its appliances, seen here on 16 August 2007, are, from left to right: Carmichael Unipower Major Foam Vehicles 38 AY 94 and PB 07 AA, Alvis Unipower Rapid Intervention Vehicle RH 10 AA.

1997 Alvis Unipower RIV of the Defence Fire and Rescue Service, with a 5,000 lpm pump, provides fire cover for the helicopters of the Army Air Corps and is seen here on 31 July 2007 at Netheravon Airfield. This airfield is the oldest in the county from which regular military flying continues. It was used by the RFC and RAF from 16 June 1913 – 31 July 1963 when the station was transferred to the army.

2006 Volvo Saxon AU 05 AB, 2000 lpm pump of the Defence Fire and Rescue Service outside the fire station of the Joint Service Military Establishment, Rudloe Manor, Corsham, on 20 August 2007. The appliance carries 75-minute long duration Drager PA 94S duel cylinder BA sets for use in the vast underground complex.

A&A.E.E. Boscombe Down Fire and Rescue Service appliances at the former main fire station on the south side of the airfield's main runway, c.1978. From left to right: Thornycroft Nubian Major Mk 9, four-wheel Range Rover RIV with 100 gallons of light water, Bedford 'B' Rescue Tender with 50lb of dry powder, Bedford Water Bowser with 500 gallons and two Bedford Foam Trucks. (John Orris collection)

1977 Thornycroft Nubian Mk 9 Major Foam Tender VHO 182R of A&A.E.E. Boscombe Down Fire and Rescue Service, on the airfield in 1991. (John Orris collection)

MOD (P.E.) Fire Service appliances at Boscombe Down, *c*.1987–88. From left to right, at the rear: three Foam Tenders, Thornycroft Nubian Major Mk 9 VHO 182R Crash 7, Thornycroft Mk 9 Version (Boscombe Down only) YMY 414H Crash 4, Thornycroft Nubian Major Mk 9 DWV 149L Crash 8. At the front: three RIV Range Rovers FCG 302S Crash 3, ELA 831J (4 wheel) and MCG 902T Crash 2. (John Orris collection)

1996 Eagle Six Major Foam Tender P65 AAA of DERA Boscombe Down Fire Service, on the airfield at Boscombe Down. (John Orris cllection)

Ex-Hampshire Fire and Rescue Service Volvo FL6 14 WrL F992 NRV serving with QinetiQ Fire and Rescue Service at Boscombe Down as Crash 4. (QinetiQ)

Crash 1 at Boscombe Down is a Gloster Saro Meteor C803 XDG Rapid Intervention Vehicle. (QinetiQ)

Crash 7 VU06 UKX, one of Boscombe Down's four Cobra Mk 2 Foam Tenders at the fire station, which opened in March 2000 on the north side of the main runway. The tower at the rear is the station watch room. (QinetiQ)

A photo call at Boscombe Down for the four Cobra Foam Tenders of QinetiQ Fire and Rescue Service:
Crash 2 VU06 UKZ, Crash 3 VU06 UKY, Crash 7 VU06 UKX and Crash 8 VU06 UKW. The aircraft
on the left is a Hawk and on the right is a Harrier. (QinetiQ)

Bibliography

Simon Rowley, *British Fire Brigades*, Forest Studio Publications, 1983.
A.W. Tovey, *Memories of the Post-War AFS in Wiltshire*, Self-published, 1992.
Peter Thorpe, *Moonraker Firemen (of the Past)*, Wiltshire Library and Museum Service, 1979.
P.J. Kelly, *Road Vehicles of the Great Western Railway*, Oxford Publishing, 1973.
Ron Henderson, *The Auxiliary Fire Service*, Nostalgia Road Publications Ltd, 2006.
Rod Priddle, *Wings over Wiltshire*, ALD Design & Print, 2003.

Other Books by the Author:

GWR to Devizes (with D.Hyde). Millstream Books, Bath, 1996.
Wings of the Brave, Wilbek & Lewbar, Devizes, 1998.
Bombers' Moon, Wilbek & Lewbar, Devizes, 1999.
On a Wing and a Prayer, Wilbek & Lewbar, Devizes, 2000.
One Step to Heaven, Wilbek & Lewbar, Devizes, 2001.
Flying without Wings, Wilbek & Lewbar, Devizes, 2002.
Shades of Blue, Wilbek & Lewbar, Devizes, 2003.
Now Fly the Shadows, Wilbek & Lewbar, Devizes, 2004.
In Clear Skies, Wilbek & Lewbar, Devizes, 2005.
Wing over Wiltshire, ALD Design & Print, Sheffield, 2003.
Adventures on the Infinite Highway, Woodfield Publishing, Bognor Regis, 2004.

Other titles published by Tempus

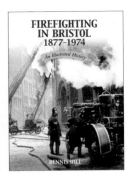

Firefighting in Bristol 1877-1974
DENNIS HILL

Charting the changes in the service from the early, horse-drawn days through innovations like the turntable ladder and fireboat, right up to 1974 when Bristol's service became part of the County of Avon Fire Brigade, Dennis Hill gives an informative and entertaining portrayal of a service on which we all depend. With over 200 photographs this book is an invaluable resource for both enthusiasts and local historians.

978-0-7524-4090-3

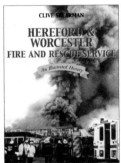

Hereford and Worcestershire Fire and Rescue Service An Illustrated History
CLIVE SHEARMAN

The combined counties of Hereford & Worcester, has a total of twenty-seven fire stations, five of which are multi-appliance stations and permanently crewed by full time personnel. This detailed and informative book is filled with descriptions of day-to-day activity by current serving staff and complemented with a wide variety of photographs.

978-0-7524-4417-4

County Durham Fire and Rescue Service An Illustrated History
RON HENDERSON

County Durham Fire and Rescue Service features over 150 archive and modern photographs of the County Durham fire service over the years. Fire historian Ron Henderson has created an evocative record detailing the post-war history of the fire service, beginning with its inception in 1948 up to the present day.

978-7524-4179-5

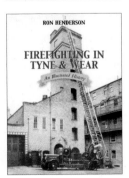

Firefighting in Tyne and Wear An Illustrated History
RON HENDERSON

This comprehensive and fully illustrated work covers times of both conflict and peace right up to the present day, including the 1974 reorganisation which created the current Tyne & Wear Fire and Rescue Service. This service now has responsibility for Newcastle, Sunderland and a further nine districts both north and south of the Tyne.

978-7524-4274-7

If you are interested in purchasing other books published by Tempus, or in case you have difficulty finding any Tempus books in your local bookshop, you can also place orders directly through our website

www.thehistorypress.co.uk